Ceramics

FROM MAGIC POTS TO MAN-MADE BONES

RUTH G. KASSINGER

Material World
Twenty-First Century Books
Brookfield, Connecticut

To Karen Kassinger

Cover photograph courtesy of Werner Forman/Art Resouce, N.Y.
Photographs courtesy of © SuperStock: pp. 4 (The Lowe Art Museum, The University of Miami), 32, 36 (Jacksonville Museum of Contemporary Art, Florida), 40 (Musée Du Louvre, Paris), 41 (Musée Du Louvre, Paris), 43, 62, 68; PhotoEdit: p. 6 (© Robert Brenner); © Bridgeman Art Library: pp. 10 (Giraudon/Lauros), 51 (Clandon Park, Surrey, UK); © Alice MacFarlane: p. 13 (top); © George Payne www.cajunimages.com: pp. 13 (bottom), 15, 34, 37, 61; © Archivo Iconografico, S.A./Corbis: p. 14; © Borromeo/Art Resource, NY: p. 17; © Werner Forman Archive/Art Resource, NY: pp. 18, 45; © Réunion des Musée Nationaux/Art Resource, NY: pp. 22, 38, 47; © Scala/Art Resource, NY: pp. 25, 57; Visuals Unlimited, Inc.: p. 29 (left © Albert J. Copley); © Corbis: p. 29 (right © W. Cody); © Tom Pantages: p. 30; © Victoria & Albert Museum, London/Art Resource, NY: pp. 49, 52; © Smithsonian American Art Museum, Washington/Art Resource, NY: p. 53; Photo Researchers, Inc.: p. 66 (© Mauro Fermariello/SPL). Map by Joe LeMonnier.

Library of Congress Cataloging-in-Publication Data
Kassinger, Ruth, 1954–
Ceramics : from magic pots to man-made bones / Ruth G. Kassinger.
p. cm. — (Material world)
Summary: Examines the discovery of pottery and ceramics and their uses throughout history, gives a scientific explanation of the properties of clay, and looks at how ceramics are used in modern technology.
Includes bibliographical references and index.
ISBN 0-7613-2108-X (lib. bdg.)
1. Ceramics—Juvenile literature. [1. Ceramics. 2. Pottery.]
I. Title. II. Series: Kassinger, Ruth, 1954-   . Material world.
TP808.2.K37 2003   666—dc21   2002011512

Published by Twenty-First Century Books
A Division of The Millbrook Press, Inc.
2 Old New Milford Road
Brookfield, Connecticut 06804
www.millbrookpress.com

*Ancient female effigy vessel
found in Costa Rica*

Contents

It's fun to make mud pies. But even if there is clay in a mud pie, kids can't make ceramics because sunlight isn't hot enough to permanently harden clay. (If a mud pie gets wet, it turns into mud again.) It takes a temperature of at least 900°F (500°C) to turn clay and water into ceramics.

CHAPTER ONE

The Beginnings

THE BEGINNINGS OF CERAMICS

As generations of little kids have discovered (and maybe once you did, too), making a mud pie is easy. First, you get some backyard dirt. Next, you mix in a little water, knead it well with your hands, and mold it into shape. Then you leave it out in the sun to bake. After a while, the mud dries, and there you have it: a hard sun-baked "pie."

For thousands of years, human beings have been using these basic mud pie ingredients and mud pie techniques to make *ceramics* (from the Greek work *keramos*, meaning "potter's clay"). Ceramics are objects made of a special—but common—kind of dirt called *clay* that has been mixed with water and then *fired* (heated to a high temperature) to make them permanently hard. Long before people learned to make fabric or paper, they learned how to shape damp clay into pots and bake them with fire.

Some inventions, such as steel or the printing press, were dreamed up at a particular time and place and then spread by people throughout the world. Others, including the boat

Before ceramic pots were invented, most people couldn't eat soups, stews, or porridges that required lengthy boiling. Once people had ceramic pots, their diets became more nutritious. Lengthy boiling breaks down the outer shells of grains and makes them easily digested. Lengthy boiling is also very effective at killing bacteria that spoil meat, so people who had ceramic pots were less likely to get sick or die from food poisoning.

Some people, including some Native American tribes, invented a way of boiling without ceramic pots. They put water in wood or leather pots, added the food to be cooked, and then dropped fire-heated stones into the water. The stones had holes in them, so people could put them in and take them out with a stick. The stones heated the water to boiling! Stone boiling had two major drawbacks: It took a long time, and the grit from the stones eventually wore down the enamel on people's teeth.

and ceramics, were invented and reinvented time and time again around the globe. No one knows for sure how people figured out that heating clay with fire would make it hard, but observant individuals would have seen the phenomenon produced accidentally.

Some ancient peoples, for instance, built their cooking fires in shallow pits in the ground to protect the flames from wind. When they dug these fire pits in dirt that contained a lot of clay, they might have seen that the fire baked the sides of the pit to hardness. Other peoples may have discovered the technique when they left a mud-lined basket too close to a fire. (People lined baskets with mud to prevent tiny objects, such as seeds, from slipping out.) If a mud-lined basket burned, the basket would go up in smoke, leaving a ceramic container behind. Or people may have made small clay figurines—just as kids make mud pies and other objects—that were accidentally burned to hardness near or in a fire.

We do know that ancient people all over the world invented *pottery* (objects, such as pots and vases, that are made from ceramics) only after they settled down in communities. Hunter-gatherers, who followed migrating herds of animals and gathered wild fruits, nuts, and grains to eat, used carved wood bowls, leather bags, empty gourds, woven baskets, or even empty ostrich egg shells as containers and cooking vessels. Ceramics would have been too heavy and too fragile for people constantly on the move.

THE FIRST POTTERY

The earliest pottery found by archaeologists was made in Japan about 10,500 B.C. Why did the Japanese invent pottery at this time? The Ice Age was just ending, and as the global climate warmed and the great sheets of ice melted, ocean levels rose. In the Japanese islands, the rising water created thousands of miles of new shoreline with numerous shallow bays and inlets. These waters were a perfect habitat for fish and shellfish, as well as the birds that lived off them. Because a greater variety of vegetation thrives in warmer climates, there was also a great increase in the number and variety of nut- and fruit-bearing trees and other edible plants and fruits.

The Japanese islands became a wonderful place for people to live. The Japanese used fishhooks and spears to catch fish and mortars and pestles to grind nuts and grains. There was so much food to eat, especially from the sea, that people could settle down instead of constantly moving to hunt animals. In fact, there was a surplus of food, and the people needed con-

This is an early piece of Japanese pottery called Jomon pottery. *The word Jomon means "cord-mark," which was how the potters decorated their containers. They took a piece of cord made from a plant and rolled it along the surface of a damp pot to create patterns. After they fired the pots, the marks remained.*

tainers to store it. They were inspired to create waterproof, fireproof ceramic containers for cooking. The weight of the pottery didn't matter because the people were settled.

Pottery next developed in the Near East (a region that includes modern Turkey, Lebanon, Jordan, Israel, Syria, Iran, and Iraq) about 6000 B.C. Near Easterners were the first to learn to cultivate crops and to domesticate (tame and raise) goats, sheep, and cattle. Once people became farmers, they not only needed containers to cook in, they also needed containers to store the surplus grain they harvested in the fall and would eat in the winter. Herders needed containers to store goats' milk.

Before inventing ceramics, Near Easterners stored their grain in baskets or in pits that they had dug in the earth and painted with plaster, a mixture of the mineral compounds lime, sand, water, and gypsum. But insects and rodents could chew through baskets or burrow into pits. Once people learned to make ceramic containers, they made them by the thousands.

EARLY POTTERY TECHNIQUES

The Jomon potters made pots using a technique called *coil construction*. A potter formed a flat piece of clay for the base of the pot. Then he or she rolled a long, thin snake of clay, formed it into a circle, and placed it on top of the base. By adding circles (coils) of clay one on top of another, the potter built the walls of the pot. Longer coils made a pot wider, while shorter coils narrowed the pot. After the basic shape of the pot was completed, the potter rubbed it inside and out with a soupy mixture of clay and water (called *slip*) to join the coils together and form a smooth surface.

Many of the ancient potters in west Asia and the Near East used a technique called *slab construction* to form pots. First, the potters pounded clay into flat slabs. Then they used slip to attach side slabs to a base slab and to each other to form a pot. Both slab and coil construction are hand-building methods.

THE POTTER'S WHEEL

The wall of a pot needs to be of an even thickness. If some parts of the wall are thicker than others, those parts will dry more slowly, and these differences in moisture levels can cause a pot to break as it is fired. Potters, therefore, need to constantly work on all sides of a pot to make sure that it is a uniform thickness. They also want to make sure the pot looks pleasing from all views.

To help ensure that their pots were uniform, ancient potters usually put their work on a mat or a slab of wood and turned the slab around so they could work on all sides without having to move themselves around the pot. About 3500 B.C., potters in the Near East figured out that if they put a stone beneath the slab or made a slab with a point under its center, the slab would turn more easily. This *turntable* allowed them to turn their work with little effort.

Not long after the invention of the turntable, potters found that if they put a lump of clay on a turntable and spun it very fast, something surprising happened: As a potter touched the spinning clay, her (or his) light touch would shape the clay. If she pressed down lightly in the center of the spinning lump, a hole would open up. With a little pressure on the inner walls of the hole, she could make a large cavity. If she put one hand on the inside wall of the pot and the other hand on the outer wall, she could make the walls of the pot rise.

The potter's wheel uses centrifugal force to work. Centrifugal force is the outward force generated by a spinning body (in this case, the potter's wheel). The potter's hands control that outward-going force, channeling the energy into shaping the clay.

In addition, as long as the clay remained exactly in the center of the fast-spinning turntable and her hand was very steady, the pot she produced would be symmetrical (exactly the same all around). With practice, potters could make pots more quickly on fast-spinning turntables than they could by hand.

Potters still use hand-building methods to make pots. The potter above is using coil construction. The potter on the right is using slab construction.

13

As Near Eastern potters began to use turntables, they made improvements to them. They found that a heavy wheel worked best because, once the potter got it spinning fast, its inertia (the tendency of objects to keep moving in the same direction) made it continue spinning longer than a lighter disk would. They also learned to carve a round hole (or socket) on the underside of the heavy wheel. The socket fit onto the spindle (a round rod) of another wheel beneath it.

True potter's wheels were being made about 3250 B.C. and continued to be used for thousands of years. The invention spread east to India, China, and Japan, and west to Europe.

This ancient Bronze Age potter's wheel was found in Syria. On the top is the lower wheel, which would have been placed on the ground or a table with its spindle pointing up. The larger part would have been placed on the wheel, with the socket covering the spindle.

Potters found that if they connected two wheels with a fixed axle (a bar joining two wheels), they could kick the lower wheel with a foot rather than spin it with a hand. That way, they had both hands free to shape the pot. Today, the foot-wheel is still very much in use, although often powered by an electric motor rather than a potter's foot.

While it was easier to make pots on a wheel, many ancient people continued to use coil and slab construction methods. The potter's wheel arrived in the Americas when the Europeans started emigrating in the sixteenth century.

EARLY FIRING TECHNIQUES

It is assumed that early pottery was fired directly in a bonfire. Although we have no physical evidence of exactly how the earliest potters fired their pots, some ancient pieces still show scorch marks made by flames. We can also guess at ancient firing techniques by looking at how potters of the Mbeere tribe in east Kenya fire pots today.

East Africans were making pottery as early as 6000 B.C. Today, women of the Mbeere tribe continue ancient pottery-making traditions. They dig clay from the earth, prepare it by removing visible grass and twigs, knead it, shape it into pots using coil construction, and decorate the pots by pressing or cutting lines into their surfaces. Then they set the pots aside for many days to ensure that they dry evenly and thoroughly and will not explode in the firing process.

Once their pots are dry, the Mbeere fire them in a shallow pit that is protected from the wind. Potters select grass and wood for fuel that will burn slowly and produce high temperatures. First, they spread wood at the bottom of the pit, pile the dried pots on top of the wood, and tie the pots together. Then they cover the pots with dry and green grass and ignite the dry grass. The dry grass burns quickly, igniting the wood beneath. The green grass (which holds a lot of moisture and therefore doesn't burn well) keeps the wood's heat from escaping. The firing takes two to three hours, and the temperature is relatively low, about 1300°F (700°C).

The earliest potters probably fired their pots as the Mbeere do today. As potters became more expert in creating different kinds of pottery and more creative in decorating their work, they wanted to avoid the scorch marks from open fires. *Kilns* (special ovens for firing pottery) solved the problem. People in the Near East were using kilns by 5700 B.C. and soon after in China. The kilns could be made of stone, earth, fired bricks, broken pottery, or a combination of these materials. Some were built into hillsides, others were freestanding and shaped like beehives. All could produce higher temperatures—and therefore more durable pottery—than an open fire. Some had two chambers, one for the fire and one for the pottery, to ensure that flames didn't scorch the pots.

In this ancient Egyptian
wood and stucco statuette, two potters
work at a simple kiln.

Archaeologists know that the Dolni Vestonice potters were capable of making ceramic objects that didn't break. They found this baked clay figurine, called the Dolni Vestonice Venus, in a hut where people lived. With her exaggerated hips and breasts, the female figure may have been a representation of a fertility goddess that women prayed to when they wanted to become pregnant.

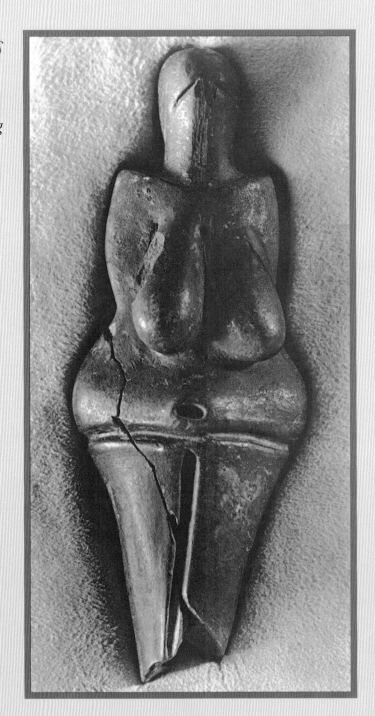

CHAPTER TWO

Myth, Magic, and Ceramics

EXPLODING CERAMICS

About 24,000 B.C., near the modern town of Dolni Vestonice in the Czech Republic, a tribe of hunter-gatherers lived on a swampy piece of land where two rivers joined. The people hunted woolly mammoths (the now-extinct species related to elephants) and other wild animals, and they gathered berries and wild plants to eat. They lived in a village of circular huts that had dirt floors and roofs made from tree branches covered with animal skins. Their clothing was made of animal skins, and they wore polished shell necklaces for jewelry.

Up the hill from the village was a special hut. Inside, a fire pit made of earth and limestone occupied the center of the dirt floor. When archaeologists uncovered the site, they found thousands of shattered pieces of baked clay animals. Another village nearby also had a fire pit surrounded by broken clay animals as well as broken clay human figures. These pieces of baked clay are the earliest examples of ceramics anywhere in the world. These ceramic figurines preceded the world's earliest pottery (made in Japan) by more than 13,000 years!

The archaeologists were amazed by how old the figurines were and also puzzled by the fact that not one single figurine was whole. How could it be that out of thousands of figurines, not one survived intact? By looking at the edges of the fragments with a powerful microscope, ceramic specialists found the answer: All the figurines suffered from thermal shock. In ceramics, thermal shock results when clay is insufficiently dried and then rapidly heated. As the remaining water in the clay turns to steam, it expands and literally explodes the baking clay.

Was it possible that the potters of Dolni Vestonice were so incompetent that they never figured out that they had to dry their figurines more thoroughly before heating them? Archaeologists don't think so. They believe that Dolni Vestonice was a meeting place for the nomadic hunting tribes in the region. They think that the potters were participating in a kind of magic ritual that came to a dramatic conclusion with the loud explosion of the figurines. Were the exploding animals symbols of the animals the people hoped to kill? Did the human figurines represent gods or perhaps their enemies? We'll never know for sure because these people lived more than 20,000 years before writing was invented, so they left no records. But it seems very likely that the exploding ceramics invoked some sort of magic.

CLAY AND THE CREATION OF MANKIND

Many ancient civilizations developed creation stories that explained how God or gods made people out of clay. The story of Genesis, which is the first book of the Christian Bible and the Jewish Torah, tells of the miracle that God performed when He "formed man out of the dust of the ground; and breathed into his nostrils the breath of life, and man became a living soul." An even older creation story is found on a clay tablet in the city of Sumer, which thrived in modern Iraq about 3000 B.C. In this story, the Sumerian god of water, Enki, makes the first men of clay. The Hopi Indians of North America tell the story of how Kokyanwuhti, the Spider Woman, scooped up clay and formed the figures of a man and a woman. Then she and Tawa, the Sun god, sang the magic Song of Life over them to give them a living spirit.

The Incas, who created a great civilization that thrived in Peru before the Spanish invaded in the sixteenth century, had a related tale. They believed that a Great Flood once covered the highest mountains and destroyed all life. After the Flood, the god Viracocha molded new people out of clay. He painted them with the features, clothes, and hairstyles of all the nations and gave the clay people their languages, songs, and the seeds they were to plant. After bringing them to life, Viracocha ordered them to travel underground and emerge at different places on Earth to start their new lives. The story not only explained creation but also how different cultures came to exist.

All these stories were conceived by people who could make ceramics. The stories convey the wonder and the power of creating something extraordinary out of the most ordinary materials, a feeling that early people had as they made ceramics.

In ancient Greek mythology, Prometheus was given the job of creating Man. He fashioned a figure out of clay, and Athena, the goddess of wisdom, breathed life into him.

THE MAGICAL POT: A KALINGA TALE

When pottery making first came to ancient villages, it must have seemed magical. Ceramic pots enabled people to cook cereals such as rice and wheat that made them stronger and healthier. William Longacre is an ethnoarchaeologist (a scientist who studies current primitive cultures as a way of understanding prehistoric cultures) who spent many years researching how pottery is made and used in the Philippines and China. One day in 1975, a man told him how the Kalinga people of the Dangtalan region of the Philippines believe pottery came to his people:

The god Kabunyan, the man said, once had a sugar mill in Sumadel. The mill was very noisy, and the noise irritated his neighbors. One night, the people attacked and killed Kabunyan's son. Kabunyan left the town, but wreaked his revenge by giving every family a pot that no matter how full they filled it with rice, they could never consume enough to feel full, thus condemning them to hunger forever.

The next morning, Kabunyan went to Dangtalan and looked for a container to cook his rice. Finding none, he made one out of clay that he dug out of the ground. The people watched the god make the pot and ever since, the storyteller concluded, the women of Dangtalan have been potters.

The first part of the story establishes the important link that people saw between having pottery and maintaining a sufficient food supply. The second part conveys how magical the making of pots seemed to primitive people: It was a god who brought pottery making to the people of Dangtalan.

MAGICAL POTTERS

In ancient times, the science behind ceramics was not understood, and success in pottery making was hit-or-miss. Potters had no thermometers to help them know when the temperature in a kiln was right or when they could safely remove their pots. Ancient potters often found that half or more of their pots broke during a firing. The ancient kilns and firing hearths that archaeologists have discovered are surrounded by huge numbers of broken pots (*potsherds*).

Ancient people were mystified by the breakage of pots in the kiln. Seemingly identical pots went into the kiln, yet some would shatter for no reason they could understand. People could never tell which pots would break and which would survive. Many people in all parts of the world concluded that evil or mischievous spirits were at work.

One of the advantages of a settled agricultural and herding existence was that farmers and herders were able to produce more food than they could eat themselves. Then they could trade their surplus crops, meat, and milk to people who had special skills, such as beekeeping, weaving, and pottery making. Because these craftspeople could use their honey, textiles, and pots to trade for food rather than produce the food themselves, they could devote all their time and energy to perfecting their crafts.

As full-time potters became more practiced and skillful, they had fewer failures in the kiln than people who only occa-

This ancient Greek mask, made of painted terra-cotta, *a reddish clay that hardens at a relatively low kiln temperature, was used to appease the spirits.*

sionally made pots. Sometimes villagers (and probably the potters themselves) came to believe that the successful potters had magical powers.

People believed that potters somehow soothed the spirits that lived in the earth, water, and fire of which pottery was made. In some cultures, potters came to be regarded as shamans (people who act as an intermediary between the supernatural and the natural worlds and perform magic) and became powerful people in their communities.

By about 600 B.C. in ancient Greece, ceramics had become an art and a profession, and potters worked together in workshops to produce large quantities of pottery in kilns. But the Greeks, too, believed that there were spirits determined to destroy some of their beautiful and sophisticated work. They hung magical masks above the kilns and recited incantations (chants) to keep the spirits from destroying their work.

Today, when the potters of the Mbeere tribe in eastern Kenya begin to collect clay for their pots, they pray to the ancestral spirits and offer them food in hopes that the spirits will allow them to collect good clay. People who carry the clay back to the village look around to make sure that no one gives the clay "the evil eye" on the way. They believe that if the clay is seen by an evil eye, the pots made from it will break during firing. Without an understanding of the chemistry and physics of ceramics, pottery making still seems like a magical process.

CHAPTER THREE
The Science of Ceramics

WHAT IS CLAY?

Billions of years ago the Earth was a fiery mass of metals and minerals. As the hot Earth cooled, molten material solidified into rock. The atmosphere of our planet cooled, too, and winds blew and rain fell. Cycles of cooling and heating made the rocks crack and break apart, and as the wind and rain scoured the rocks, the rocks began to wear away.

Certain rocks contained the mineral feldspar, which further eroded and broke down into smaller particles containing potassium, aluminum, and silicon. The potassium particles dissolved in water and washed away. The particles made from aluminum and silicon combined with oxygen to form the compounds alumina and silica. When the alumina and silica united with water, the result was kaolinite. A little kaolinite is found in many kinds of soil, but when there are high concentrations of kaolinite, the resulting earthy material is a kind of clay called *kaolin*.

Clay is a general term for soft, malleable material that is rich in kaolinite. Clay almost always also contains other minerals such as quartz, titanium, mica, calcium, feldspar, and iron, as well as microscopic particles of organic (carbon-containing) material such as leaves and lichens. The composition of a clay determines at what temperature it will become hard during firing. The composition of a particular clay also determines its physical properties. *Fireclays*, for example, have iron in them and are used to make bricks. *Earthenware* clays contain minerals that allow them to become hard at relatively low temperatures, but that make the resulting ceramics fragile and porous. *Ceramists* (people who make ceramic articles) often mix various clays, as well as other minerals, to make a clay for a particular use.

Potassium, aluminum, silicon, and oxygen are chemical elements, substances that consist of atoms of only one kind and that cannot be broken down by chemical means into other substances. When the atoms of two or more elements are chemically combined in fixed proportions, the combinations are called compounds.

WATER AND CLAY

Water is an essential part of clay. Water is a molecule (a combination of atoms) made of two atoms of hydrogen combined with one atom of oxygen. (The chemical symbol for water is H_2O.) In kaolinite, two molecules of water ($2H_2O$) are chemically bound to one molecule of alumina (Al_2O_3) and two molecules of silica ($2SiO_2$).

Two common clays are pictured here. The white clay is kaolin and is used to make a fine ceramic called porcelain, which is fired at high temperatures. Kaolin has very few impurities. The red clay probably has a high content of iron oxides, which turns it red. Some clays are yellow, which usually means that they contain yellow iron oxide. Gray and beige clays are colored by the organic material in them. Potters can add chemicals to clay to turn it green, blue, yellow, and purple.

What does it mean when we say molecules are chemically bound to each other?

All atoms are composed of a dense central part called the nucleus. In the nucleus are particles called protons, which carry a positive (+) electrical charge, and neutrons, which carry no electrical charge. Surrounding and circling the nucleus are electrons, which carry a negative (–) charge. In an electrically neutral atom, there is an equal number of protons and electrons.

In all atoms, electrons arrange themselves in shells at various distances around a nucleus. Each shell can hold a certain number of electrons. For example, the first shell can hold up to two electrons, and the second shell can hold up to eight electrons. When the outermost shell of an atom has its full complement of electrons, it is chemically stable.

The electrons in the outermost shell of an incomplete atom, called valence electrons, play a very important role in making chemical compounds. Valence electrons are transferred from the outer shell of one atom to the outer shell of another or shared among atoms so that the atoms have complete outer shells. When valence atoms are transferred or shared among atoms, we say that those atoms are chemically bonded. In clay, water is chemically bonded to alumina and silica.

Water is essential to clay in another way. Clay also contains water that is not chemically bonded. Kaolinite is composed of very fine crystals of alumina silicates that are far smaller than the eye can see. Those crystals attach to one another in sheets that are only one crystal deep. Between each crystal sheet is a layer of water. The water

A simple example of chemical bonding is water (H_2O). Oxygen atoms have two electrons in their inner shell and six valence electrons in their second shell. Therefore, an oxygen atom tends to attract atoms that can share or add two electrons so that its outer shell is filled with eight electrons. Hydrogen atoms have only one electron in its inner (and only) shell. Therefore, two hydrogen atoms easily become chemically bonded to one oxygen atom, adding a total of two electrons to complete oxygen's outer shell.

allows the sheets of crystals to slide easily over each other. It is this water that makes unfired clay so plastic (easy to shape).

DRYING AND FIRING

The first step in turning clay into a ceramic is to let a clay object dry. When the water that allowed the crystal sheets to slide past each other has disappeared, the crystal sheets touch each other. Because the crystals are three-dimensional, when they lie flat against each other their surfaces engage and become locked together, something like the way two pieces of Velcro lock.

Remember slip, the soupy mixture of clay and water that potters use to finish and smooth the surface of a coil pot? Its name describes just how it feels: slippery. Slip is made by adding extra water to clay. The added water in slip allows the crystal sheets to slide even more easily over each other.

■ ■ ■

Clay is a suspension, a physical state in which particles of matter are evenly distributed—but not dissolved—in a fluid. How does kaolinite stay so evenly mixed in water? The particles of clay are bombarded on all sides by water molecules that keep them from settling out.

A piece of ceramic must be air-dried before it is put into the kiln. If it isn't, the moisture between the crystals in the clay will expand, turn to steam, and blow the ceramic apart. The people at Dolni Vestonice who made the exploding figurines 26,0000 years ago (see Chapter Two) took advantage of this fact and put their figurines into the fire when they were still damp.

Next, the potter fires the dried clay object. At about 600°F (318°C), the last traces of water between the crystals evapo-

The pink pots have *just been made. The paler pots have dried for several days and are ready for firing.*

rate. As the temperature rises further, the water that is chemically bonded in the kaolinite begins to be driven off as steam. When the kiln reaches about 850°F (458°C), all the chemically bonded water has disappeared, too.

As the kiln temperature rises to about 900°F (about 500°C), depending on the composition of the clay, a process called *sintering* begins. During sintering, the molecules of silica and alumina soften and collapse together to partially fill the spaces left by the water that has been driven off. The alumina and the silica become interlaced, somewhat like the way straw in a basket is woven together. If a potter fires a clay object until the silica and alumina have sintered, the fired clay object will be hard and useful. It will no longer absorb water and can never return to clay again. The bonfires used to fire ancient ceramics achieved temperatures that sintered ceramics.

At about 1650°F (900°C), another chemical process called *vitrification* begins. Now the silica, as well as impurities such as mica and iron oxides, actually liquefy (become liquid) and form a noncrystalline, glassy substance that flows around the remaining alumina molecules. The higher the temperature, the more glassy the ceramic object becomes. The glassier the object, the harder and more rigid it will be. *Porcelain* is a very glassy ceramic. If you tap a porcelain plate, it will sound a clear tone, almost like ringing a bell.

IS IT DONE YET?

When you put unbaked cookies into an oven, it takes time for the heat to cook them. Not all cookies take exactly the same amount of time to cook: Delicate sugar cookies may cook more quickly than heavy oatmeal cookies. To determine if cookies are properly baked, cooks first look at an oven thermometer to make sure that the oven is the correct temperature for baking. They also look at the color of the cookies to see if they're nicely browned on top. They may also poke a toothpick into a cookie to see if the inside is still doughy.

Like cookies, pots are not instantly "cooked." Firing takes time. But how do potters know when ceramics are done?

As a piece of pottery dries and then is fired, it shrinks. A piece of fired pottery will be about 15 to 20 percent smaller than it was when the potter shaped it.

These pyrometric cones tell the potter what effect the heat of the kiln is having on the clay objects inside.

Ancient potters judged the temperature inside their kilns by color: As the temperature rose, the color of the kiln's interior walls changed from red to orange to yellow. Today, potters look at a kiln thermometer called a *pyrometer* (*pyro* means "heat" and *meter* means "measure" in Greek) to see if the kiln has reached the right temperature.

It isn't practical to poke a toothpick into a piece of pottery to see if it's properly fired on the inside. Instead, potters use a numbered series of ceramic *pyrometric cones* to determine the effect that the heat of the kiln has had on the baking clay. Each cone is made of a different combination of ceramic ingredients and is known to collapse under certain conditions of heat and time. Potters place a series of numbered cones in the kiln along with the clay objects to be fired. They watch what happens to the cones to determine what is happening to the pottery. As the kiln temperature rises over time, one cone after another slowly slumps over to the side. A potter knows, for example, that an object made of nearly pure kaolin will be finished when cone No. 12 is bent halfway over.

It takes many hours and sometimes many days to slowly heat and then slowly cool ceramics. Most materials expand when heated and contract when cooled. Ceramic products are not very elastic, meaning they can't stretch very much without breaking. If a ceramic pot is heated or cooled too quickly, it suffers from thermal shock and cracks or shatters.

AFTER FIRING: ADDING COLOR, DESIGN, AND TEXTURE

Have you ever passed by a stretch of wet cement in a sidewalk? Isn't it tempting to write your initials, leave a handprint, or make a design in the cement? It seems to be part of human nature to express ourselves by embellishing the surfaces of the objects around us.

Even the earliest potters felt this way. Before firing a pot, they used their fingers, sticks, or strings to add texture and pattern to its moist blank surface. Sometimes the designs they created expressed a potter's individuality and identity. Sometimes potters used designs that identified the pot as

The potter created the *facial features on this pre-Columbian Peruvian parrot-shaped vessel by cutting into the clay.*

being made by their tribe. Decorated pottery became an art form, as appreciated for its beauty and expression as painting and sculpture.

Early potters soon discovered that they could apply *glazes* to their work to give them color as well as additional design and texture. Glazes are made of finely ground minerals suspended in a liquid. When glazes are fired, they become a glassy coating and can also seal the porous surface of pottery so that liquid can't escape

Glazes can be brushed, poured, or sprayed on a pot, and they can be added before or after a pot has been fired. If a glaze is added to a fired pot, the potter fires the pot again after glazing. Potters often use more than one glaze. Sometimes they add *overglazes* on top of a primary glaze. Overglazes are fired at a lower temperature than the glaze so that the primary glaze will not melt again. As you will see in Chapter Four, ceramics makers have discovered a multitude of glazes that help them create a nearly infinite variety of beautiful and striking effects.

A modern potter dips a fired pot into a glaze.

To decorate this late Stone Age terra-cotta beaker, the Susa potter used an ibex design. An ibex is a kind of antelope.

Milestones in Ceramic Art

ARTISTIC BEGINNINGS: 9000 TO 2500 B.C.

During the time known as the Neolithic period of history, which stretched from about 9000 B.C. to the beginning of written languages about 2500 B.C., people in Africa, Europe, and Asia poured much of their artistic creativity into ceramics. Archaeologists guess that women produced much of the world's pottery at this time. By the end of the Neolithic period, many cultures had potter's wheels and kilns and were able to produce a great variety of containers. In ancient Japan, the shape of Jomon pottery became more and more ornate. In the Near East, potters painted their work with geometric patterns and stylized animals. In the fourth millennium B.C., potters in the town of Susa, in what is today Iraq, made particularly fine wares, some with elegant shapes and eggshell-thin walls.

BRONZE AGE CERAMICS: 2500 TO 1000 B.C.

With the invention of copper smelting and bronze manufacture in the sophisticated civilizations of the Near East, pottery became a less important medium (the means by which an idea is conveyed) for artistic expression. Artists focused their attention on these new metals instead. Nonetheless, skilled craftsmen made the important discovery of glazes during this period, and brighter colors and shiny surfaces added to the vitality of ceramics. The Egyptians made dramatic use of glazes on small sculptures. When they dusted the surface of a clay object with copper oxide and then fired the object, it turned a beautiful turquoise!

This humorous hippo statue, affectionately known as "Wilbur," was made in Egypt about 1700 B.C. His body is decorated with leaves and flowers, and he is glazed with a copper oxide glaze. Does he seem to be smiling at you?

GREEK CERAMICS: 1000–200 B.C.

Ancient Greeks preferred that the surface of their containers be smooth. Among the most common containers they made were amphoras, which held wine, olive oil, and other liquids; kraters, used for mixing water and wine; and hydras, which had three handles and held water. These and other containers, plates, cups, and goblets were made in workshops that produced thousands of pieces each year. The workshops generally employed ten to twenty potters who made the containers as well as artists who decorated the work. The potters and artists were well respected in Greek society. We know some of them by name because they signed their work.

While the shapes of the Greek containers are pleasing to the eye, it is the detailed designs on their surfaces that make them so remarkable. Artists often painted scenes from Greek mythology, literature, and history on their work, so the pots not only were beautiful but also told a story. Pottery made in Athens around 600 B.C. was often of the "black-figure"

This ancient Greek amphora dating from 1000–900 B.C. is in the red-on-black style.

style. On these pieces, potters applied a shiny black paint to a red-orange surface. By the mid-500s B.C., pottery made in the Greek city of Corinth became very popular. These "red-figure" pieces had the opposite pattern, red figures on a black background.

A CERAMIC ARMY: 220 B.C.

In the spring of 1974, some peasants were digging a new well near the town of Xi'an in China's Shaanxi province. As they dug into the earth, their shovels hit broken clay pottery and some rusty bronze arrowheads. They carted the "trash" home, using the pottery as containers and selling the bronze as scrap metal.

Fortunately, some researchers at the nearby Shaanxi Archaeology Institute learned about the finds and stepped in. The peasants, it turned out, had made one of the most spectacular archaeological discoveries of the twentieth century. When archaeologists got to work, they uncovered an army made out of ceramics! So far (and the excavation still isn't complete), eight thousand full-size soldiers carrying weapons and riding or leading horses have been found.

This huge ceramic army was created at the direction of Emperor Qin (pronounced Chin), who ascended the throne at the age of thirteen in 246 B.C. and ruled until his death in 210 B.C. Qin was a ruthless but very successful ruler who conquered six warring states to unify China in 221 B.C. Under his rule, the Chinese formed a centralized government, built roads and canals, completed the famous Great Wall, developed a national currency, and formalized a written language. The word *China* comes from the emperor's name.

These life-size terra-cotta soldiers were buried
with Chinese Emperor Qin in 210 B.C.

Qin made a lot of enemies in his life (assassins tried to kill him three times) and was anxious about what would happen to him in the afterlife. He decided to re-create his army in clay so that it could protect him after his death. He ordered his craftsmen to duplicate all his soldiers and their horses and place them in trenches in an underground mausoleum (tomb). As a result, no two soldiers look alike.

The soldiers were made out of terra-cotta. The bodies, hands, and heads of the soldiers were made separately. A half-finished head and hands were pasted with slip onto a soldier's body. Then the head was smeared with clay, and the artist pinched, pasted, and carved the surface to give each soldier his own unique features. Colored glazes, most of which have since worn away, gave the soldiers and their mounts a lifelike appearance.

SOUTH AMERICAN CERAMICS: A.D. 500–1000

The Romans inherited and built on the rich tradition of Greek pottery, but after the fall of the Roman Empire about A.D. 500, there was a long pause in the development of European pottery. At the same time, however, pottery in the Near East and Middle East, in China, and in South America was reaching new artistic heights. In particular, in the area that is today southern Mexico, Guatemala, and northern Belize, the great Maya Indian civilization was producing striking ceramics.

The ancient Maya had settled in villages and cultivated crops of corn, beans, and squash as early as 1500 B.C. By A.D. 500 they had built an elaborate civilization with densely populated cities containing palaces, pyramids of stone, and impressive temples. They developed a written language, which they used to write on books made from the inner bark of trees. They made sophisticated observations of the sun and planets and could predict solar eclipses. Their goldsmiths and coppersmiths fashioned delicate jewelry, and their sculptors chiseled stone into elaborate sculptures. The Maya also produced distinctive and finely painted pottery and clay sculpture.

This Mayan figure of a woman writing was found on the island of Jaina.

One of the most popular forms for Mayan pottery was a tall cylindrical jar. The jars were painted in reds, browns, and yellows and often portrayed scenes from Mayan life and mythology. (The Mayans worshiped numerous gods of nature.) Mayan potters also crafted small sculptures called Jaina figures. The figures reflected the people and their occupations at the time, including warriors with their shields and priests in feathered headdresses. Today, the Jaina figures are valued not only for their beauty but also for the information they give us about Mayan life more than a thousand years ago.

ISLAMIC CERAMICS: A.D. 1000–1300

By A.D. 750, about a century after the Prophet Muhammad's death, the followers of Islam had conquered a large part of the globe—from Spain across Central Asia to India—and created a new Arab Muslim Empire. Potters in the Arab world developed new styles that made their work unique. Islamic potters often incorporated poetry or verses from the Koran, the sacred book of Islam, into their designs. Many Islamic potters used geometric designs on their work because their religion restricted the use of animal and human images. Some poured their creative energy into decorating tiles that covered walls and floors in a ceramic tapestry of color and pattern.

In the ninth century, they invented a new glaze called *luster*, which is a special metallic paint. Potters painted luster on the surface of a fired pot and then returned it to the kiln for a second firing at a relatively low temperature. The resulting glaze shone like gold, silver, or copper and sometimes had a spectacular shimmery effect called iridescence.

MAJOLICA: THE EUROPEAN RENAISSANCE

Ceramic artistry flourished between 1400–1700 in the Near East, the Far East, and Europe. Each country's potters developed their own distinctive style of pottery. In Italy, potters made *majolica*, an earthenware pottery that is glazed with a mixture of lead and tin. Majolica originated in Mesopotamia (part of modern Iraq) and spread westward. "Tin-glazed" pottery generally has a smooth white surface that makes a good background for designs with eye-popping colors. The della Robbia family in Florence, Italy, produced large and ornate pieces of majolica sculpture that were used to decorate the exteriors of buildings as well as the interiors of churches. French potters created tin-glazed wares known as *faience*. Bernard Palissy, a sixteenth-century French stained-glass maker, produced faience platters and

This faience platter by the sixteenth-century French craftsman Bernard Palissy features a snake and other creatures against a blue background.

dishes on which highly realistic three-dimensional snakes, frogs, and fish seemed to breathe and wriggle. In Holland and Britain, potters created tin-glazed ware known as *delft*. Delft potters started by imitating the blue and white Chinese porcelains that reached Dutch shores by the millions in the early 1600s. Later, they added other colors.

PORCELAIN: 1600–1800

In the seventeenth century, Europeans were introduced to an astonishing new ceramic—porcelain. Porcelain vases, plates, and other objects were bright white and highly glossy. Porcelain plates could be made so thin that they were translucent, meaning that some light could pass through. For people accustomed to sturdy tin-glazed earthenware, the delicacy of porcelain was stunning. The beautiful porcelain wares came from China, brought back by European traders. European kings and noblemen (the only people wealthy enough to afford the costly Chinese porcelain) collected it. Many palaces in Europe had special rooms to display the owner's collection.

Chinese potters discovered how to make porcelain about A.D. 700. During the Sung dynasty (960–1279) porcelain factories under the direction of the emperors produced great quantities of porcelain for the imperial palaces. During the Ming dynasty (1368–1644), imperial potters produced a pure-white and blue porcelain that became world renowned for its technical and artistic refinement. Factories during the Ming dynasty employed more than 100,000 craftsmen who labored at more than a thousand kilns.

Running dragons decorate this Ming dynasty
porcelain flask from the early fifteenth century.

In the late seventeenth century, it dawned on European collectors and entrepreneurs (enterprising business owners) that they might make a lot of money if they could make porcelain themselves. But how? The Chinese held the secret of porcelain very closely.

Over the years, Europeans attempted to discover the secret. Travelers to China secretly collected various clays as well as tales of how porcelain was made. In their attempts to re-create porcelain, European potters added various materials to their clay. They tried adding ground glass to make it translucent. They tried adding shells, bones, and even talcum powder to make it white. Nothing worked, however, and for a hundred years the Chinese were able to keep the secret of porcelain.

In 1701 the king of Poland, Augustus the Strong, was desperate: His country's treasury was nearly empty of gold and silver. Like other people of his era, he believed it was possible to make gold through a process called alchemy. (Alchemy was the pseudoscience of attempting to turn metals like lead into gold.) So he took German alchemist Johann Friedrich Böttger prisoner, locked him up in a dank laboratory in his castle, and forced him to try to make gold. Of course, Böttger couldn't make gold: Gold is an element and can't be artificially created (except at great expense and in microscopic quantities with a nuclear reactor). With his life hanging in the balance, Böttger turned his efforts to creating porcelain instead, which had become so costly that its secret was just as valuable as the secret of making gold. In 1708, Böttger finally created porcelain.

The secret, Böttger discovered, lay in using the right ingredients and kiln firing at very high temperatures. Chinese porcelain was made with kaolin. When it is fired, kaolin turns pure white. But Böttger guessed that another ingredient was needed to give fired kaolin its translucence. After thousands of experiments, he found that ingredient: It was alabaster, a fine-grained version of a white mineral called gypsum, which is a chemical compound of calcium, sulfur, and water.

Böttger went on to produce porcelain in the king's factory in Meissen (Germany). At first, Meissen designers made pieces that imitated the styles of Chinese porcelain. But soon, Meissen artists such as Johann Horoldt and Johann Joachim Kändler were producing their own unique works, including beautiful sets of tableware and elaborate figurines arranged in scenes such as ladies and gentlemen playing musical instruments or a gentleman being served tea. It didn't take long before other potters learned the secret of porcelain, and porcelain factories sprang up across Europe.

Johann Joachim Kändler created this Meissen figurine of a poultry seller around 1750.

William Morris, founder of the Arts and Crafts Movement, created these decorative floral tiles in the nineteenth century.

MODERN CERAMICS

The production of ceramics became industrialized in the 1800s. Mass-production factories took over the production of everyday ceramics. Thousands of identical objects could be made in one day in this way. This was not a period of great originality in ceramics, and many of the factories made copies of older styles. But by the end of the nineteenth century, the English designer William Morris, reacting to the lack of quality of the mass production, promoted a revival of individual craftsmanship that became known as the Arts and Crafts Movement. His ideas inspired English potters, and the movement spread throughout Europe and to the United States.

The twentieth century brought a flowering of creativity in ceramics. Universities, as well as art schools, developed courses of study in ceramics. Today, the craft continues to thrive. In the United States, thousands of

This amusing stoneware piece by the modern American potter Peter Voulkos is called "Rocking Pot."

professional *studio potters* (potters who make handcrafted pottery) make a living in ceramic artwork.

Ceramics also took an entirely new direction in the twentieth century. Ceramics have always had utilitarian (useful) functions—for storing food, containing liquids, and holding flowers, for example—as well as an artistic one. When industrial ceramists began to experiment with the chemical composition of ceramics, they found some wonderful new uses for this ancient material.

CHAPTER FIVE

Advanced Ceramics

NEW DEFINITIONS

Modern scientists have broadened the traditional definition of ceramics as new materials were invented in the twentieth century. Now ceramics are defined as any material composed in large part of inorganic, nonmetallic substances. This is a broad definition that includes all solid materials that aren't metal, plastic, or organic (made from plants or animals). The broad definition covers traditional pottery and tiles as well as glass and cement. It also covers what ceramics engineers call *advanced ceramics*, materials that are made from mineral compounds that our ancestors never knew.

SILICON NITRIDE CERAMICS

If you strike a ceramic teacup with a hammer, it will undoubtedly break. The hammer blow breaks the bonds between the atoms of the ceramic and pulls them apart. You applied too much stress to the cup.

Engineers identify three kinds of stress: compressive, bending, and tension. Compressive stress is the kind that forces material into a smaller space: What a trash compactor does is a good example of compressive stress. Bending stress is what happens when you snap a pencil in half. Tension is the kind of stress that pulls a material apart. When you hook a fish and it pulls on your line, the fish is applying tension to your fishing line.

Ceramic products, including traditional pottery, react well to compressive stress. You could put a ceramic teacup upside down and stand on it. (But don't try it with a good cup, just in case the cup has a tiny crack that your weight will cause to spread.) Ceramic bricks and concrete make good building materials because they stand up well to compressive stress. But traditional ceramics don't respond well to bending stress and tension. They also don't respond well to the stress of rapid temperature changes.

Remember that clay is made primarily of silicon and aluminum atoms combined with oxygen? In the 1960s engineers began to develop a new kind of ceramics made of silicon and nitrogen combined with oxygen. Even though silicon makes up about 28 percent of the Earth's crust and nitrogen makes up about 80 percent of the Earth's atmosphere, these two elements do not naturally combine.

Nonetheless, scientists found that when they heated silicon and nitrogen to over 2200°F (1204°C), they could make the two elements chemically combine. The new advanced ceramic, *silicon nitride*, is more resistant to stress than any other ceramic. It also withstands high temperatures and is resistant to thermal shock.

This clay brick wall was built by the Babylonians around 570 B.C. Sun-baked clay bricks were used by people in the Near East beginning in the Neolithic period. The Mesopotamians built the first sun-baked brick arch in the city of Ur around 4000 B.C. Later, people discovered that fire-baked brick was more durable and used it when they could.

Concrete, another ceramic material, is a more modern invention. English inventor Joseph Aspdin mixed limestone and clay, which, when burned and ground together, produced a hard, durable substance known as *Portland cement*. This modern invention has ancient roots, however. The ancient Egyptians made a substance of lime and gypsum that resembled modern concrete and used it to cover brick and stone structures to give them a smooth coating.

Ceramics made of silicon nitride have found a use in certain jet and other gas turbine engine parts. When a jet engine is first started, it goes from ordinary air temperature to about 1800°F (1000°C) in a few seconds. Jet engine parts are also subject to great tension: up to 40,000 psi (pounds per square inch) or the equivalent of the pressure of ten cars balanced on a 1-inch-diameter cable! They also have to resist the corrosion from the high-temperature gases. Silicon nitride parts meet these tests.

Ball bearings are small spheres that allow two surfaces to pass over each other without generating a lot of friction and destructive heat. Ball bearings are essential for engines as well as drills and other devices with rotary (turning) parts. You can also find them in car and bicycle wheels, swivel chairs, and in-line skates.

Silicon nitride is used for the ball bearings of the turbo pumps of the space shuttle because they can function in extreme temperatures. Silicon nitride bearings are also used in racing cars such as the Thrust SSC car, which achieved a top speed of more than 700 miles (1,126 kilometers) per hour.

Ball bearings traditionally have been made out of steel. But silicon nitride bearings are now taking the place of steel in certain aerospace, medical, and industrial machines. Silicon nitride bearings are three times harder than steel ball bearings and can be polished to such a smooth finish that they produce significantly less friction than steel bearings and wear far longer. They also weigh less than half as much as steel bearings of the same size, which means less energy is needed to turn them. Between 15 and 20 million silicon nitride ball bearings were made in 1996!

Silicon nitride is also an excellent material for cutting. Spinning silicon nitride blades are used to cut and shape cast iron and other metal alloys. The blades survive the 2000°F (1093°C) of heat generated by the friction between the metal and the ceramic.

Ceramic particles are also used within metals. By adding silicon nitride particles or silicon carbide fibers to a metal, engineers can produce a composite (a material made up of two different types of materials) that is stronger than the metal alone yet weighs less. Such composites are attractive to the aerospace and automobile industries, which are always looking for ways to make planes and cars lighter and therefore more fuel efficient.

CERAMICS AND ELECTRONICS

The electrons that circle an atom's nucleus (see Chapter Three) are responsible for electricity. When electrons move through metal wires, electricity flows. The amount of electricity that flows through the wires is called the current. The force that builds up in the battery or generator that pushes the electricity through the wires is known as voltage. The pressure and flow of electricity, its voltage and current, need to be regulated.

Electricity and water are somewhat alike: Sometimes you want a gush of water (when you're using a hose to put out a fire) and sometimes you need a trickle (when you're filling a teaspoon from a faucet). If you want a gush of electricity, you need a device called a conductor, made of material through which electricity easily passes. If you want a trickle of electricity, you need a resistor, a material that allows electricity to flow, but only with difficulty. Sometimes you don't want any electricity to flow, and you need an insulator. The chemical composition of ceramics can be manipulated to produce conductors, resistors, and insulators.

Ceramics have been used as insulators to carry electrical power safely for more than a hundred years. You can see a ceramic insulator if you look at the outside of the socket of a lamp or lighting fixture. The ceramic of the socket ensures that electricity flows into the bulb, not into the lamp. If you look carefully at the high-voltage power lines that are carried on tall metal towers, you will see ceramics there, too. The wires never touch the towers: Ceramic insulators come between the towers and the wires to prevent electricity from traveling down the tower and hurting someone. Ceramic insulators also protect objects from heat. The space shuttle is covered in ceramic tiles that protect it from the high temperatures generated by friction as the shuttle travels through the Earth's atmosphere.

Ceramic resistors control the amount of electricity that flows through a wire. You can find resistors in electric ovens and toasters. They limit the amount of electricity that passes through the metal wires that cook your food.

In the last fifty years or so, a special kind of ceramic called a *semiconductor* has been essential to the phenomenal growth of electronics. A semiconductor falls between an insulator and a conductor, allowing some electricity to flow. In the late 1940s,

Ceramic insulators prevent electricity from traveling from power lines to towers and to the ground.

Ceramic tiles protect the space shuttle from frictional heat.

scientists at Bell Laboratories in the United States discovered that a piece of germanium (a chemical element similar to silicon) could amplify electricity and replace the large and fragile glass vacuum tubes used in radios. They called these semiconducting ceramics transistors. In the 1950s computer engineers began to use transistors to store information (conveyed as a pulse of electricity) inside a computer.

Engineers have been able to shrink the size of transistors and other electrical components to microscopic size and to link millions of them together in a tiny piece of silicon. That piece of silicon is known as a *silicon chip*, or simply a *chip*. Today, these chips are the brains of computers, printers, fax machines, microwave ovens, automobile control systems, digital cameras, and heart pacemakers.

PIEZOELECTRIC CERAMICS

Certain natural crystals have a remarkable property: If you apply a light pressure to them, they give off an electrical pulse. These crystals are piezoelectric (*piezo*—pronounced pie-ee'-zoh—means pressure, so these crystals produce electricity when they are pressed). In the 1880s, Pierre and Jacques Curie were among the first scientists to study piezoelectric crystals, using natural crystals as well as crystals they made from salt solutions.

By 1930 engineers were making microphones with *piezoelectric ceramics*. When you speak into a microphone, your voice produces sound waves that are carried by air and make a tiny membrane vibrate (just the way tapping on a drum makes a drum sound). The membrane, called a diaphragm, transmits the sound waves to a piezoelectric ceramic, which then converts the waves into electrical pulses. The pulses can then be manipulated, amplified, and transmitted to a speaker where they are reconverted to sound waves.

Early piezoelectric ceramics were made from single salt crystals. In 1941 an engineer named R. B. Gray invented an advanced ceramic made up of tiny crystals of barium, titanium, and oxygen. This *polycrystalline* (meaning "many crystals") *ceramic* was stronger and didn't dissolve in water as salt crystals do. Today, engineers use a polycrystalline ceramic made of lead, zirconium, and oxygen, which is particularly sensitive to the lightest of pressures.

Piezoelectric ceramics are used in sonar devices that detect the location of objects underwater. The sonar device sends out sound waves via a piece of piezoelectric ceramic called a transducer. When the sound waves hit an object, they bounce back and are picked up again by the transducer. Because sound waves travel at a known speed through water, it is possible to calculate the distance from the transducer to the object. Ocean cartographers (mapmakers) rely on data produced by piezoelectric transducers that bounce sound waves off the ocean floor.

Construction engineers use piezoelectric ceramics to detect faults within building materials, such as steel. If a steel beam is flawless, sound waves sent by a transducer will pass through the beam. If there is a crack or hole inside the steel, however, the flaw will reflect the sound waves. Until piezoelectric ceramic inspection was invented, it was impossible to detect flawed materials—until a building or a bridge collapsed.

If you own a watch that you don't need to wind up, then you own a piece of piezoelectric ceramic! Inside a "quartz watch" is a tiny slice of quartz crystal that has been cut in such a way that it is piezoelectric. When the electricity produced by a watch battery is applied to the slice of quartz, it vibrates at a constant frequency (rate) of several thousands of vibrations per second. The number of vibrations determines the time displayed on the face of the watch. Quartz watches are much more accurate than mechanical watches that use springs, levers, and gears.

Piezoelectric ceramics could be in your inkjet printer, too. One kind of inkjet printer has a piezoelectric crystal at the back of each of its ink reservoirs. When an electric impulse is sent to the crystal, it flexes and forces a drop of ink out of the nozzle. The tiny fluctuations in the printer's crystals produce very small and perfectly formed dots of color.

BIOCERAMICS

In 1967 Larry Hench, a ceramic engineer at the University of Florida, was on his way by plane to a conference on materials. Seated next to him on the plane was a colonel who had just returned from fighting in the Vietnam war. The colonel told Hench about the many soldiers who had been injured in battle and had needed metal and plastic implants to repair bones. Many of those implants, the colonel reported, were being rejected by the soldiers' bodies, which meant that soldiers' limbs had to be amputated. Would Hench look into ceramics as an alternative material for implants?

Hench was intrigued and inspired. He soon concocted a new material called Bioglass made of glass, calcium, and phosphorus. Because the body is full of calcium and phosphorus, Bioglass was not rejected by the body. In fact, it bonded well to bone and tissue.

Hench's work inspired a new class of materials called *bioceramics* that are compatible with the human body and are used in repairing or replacing body parts. Unlike plastic or metal, which as they wear down release minute particles of plastic and metal that can irritate and inflame joints, bioceramics remain intact for a long time. Some bioceramics also stimulate the regrowth of bone and tissue and then are slowly absorbed into the body, leaving the new natural tissue in their place.

This porous material is made *of hydroxyapatite ceramic, a form of bioceramic used in bone reconstruction.*

Artificial eyes are now made of a bioceramic. Not only does the bioceramic eye look natural, it bonds to tissue in the eye socket. This means that the eye muscle becomes attached to the artificial eye, which then moves naturally as the person looks around. Before bioceramics, artificial eyes were made of glass. A glass eye was noticeable because it remained in a fixed position.

Ceramics are used in many other medical and dental devices, including pacemakers (which regulate the heart's rhythm), kidney dialysis machines (which cleanse blood of impurities), respirators (which help patients who cannot breathe on their own), dental caps, and dental bridges.

ARTIFICIAL GEMSTONES

Scientists in the 1800s discovered that precious rubies were made of alumina (one of the chief ingredients of clay) with a trace amount of chromium. In 1902, French professor A. V. L. Verneuil managed to melt a pure powder of alumina with a little chromium oxide by using an extremely high temperature torch to produce a synthetic (man-made) ruby. Later, he melted alumina, titanium, and iron to make a synthetic blue sapphire. Today, many artificial gemstones are made from ceramics.

Making artificial ceramic gemstones today is big business. *Cubic zirconia* (made from molten zirconium oxide) is very popular. Without color added, it looks like a diamond. When a little vanadium is added to the molten zirconium oxide, a green crystal results; when cobalt is added, the crystal turns lilac. A full spectrum of colors can be made.

Real or fake? *Many people would have difficulty distinguishing these cubic zirconia pieces from real diamonds.*

Synthetic crystals are not just beautiful but are essential for laser technology. Lasers use synthetic crystals to produce light that is monochromatic (all one color) and coherent (meaning all its light waves are lined up one on top of another so that the light is highly concentrated). Laser light is used in eye surgery, missile guidance systems, to play CDs, and in the bar code readers at the grocery store.

THE FUTURE

Ceramics is a magical material. From heavy gray blocks of concrete to clear light-filled gemstones, from ancient fire-baked pots to bioceramic bones, ceramics can take almost any shape. Scientists and engineers are now developing ceramic solar cells that we will be able to use at home to generate energy without pollution. They are working to see if a Bioglass pill will prevent older people from developing the debilitating bone disease called osteoporosis. Ceramics will increasingly find its way into airplane parts, making air travel safer. There is no material on Earth with greater potential than ceramics.

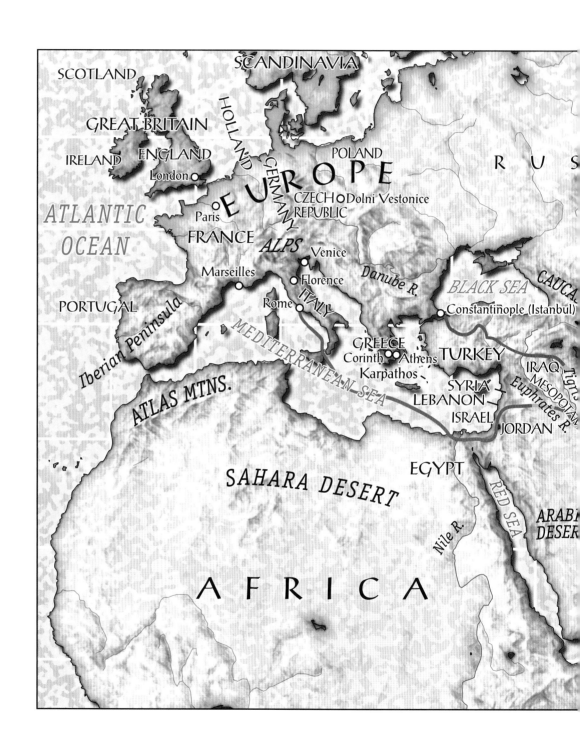

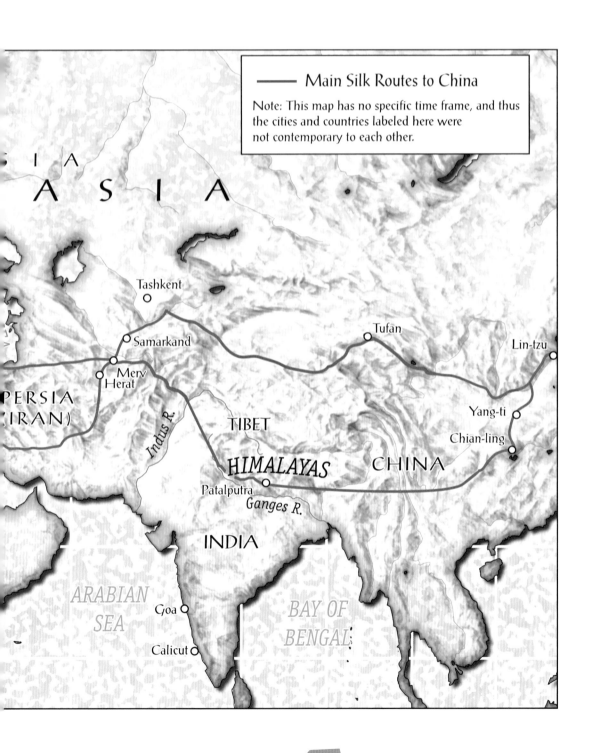

Main Silk Routes to China

Note: This map has no specific time frame, and thus the cities and countries labeled here were not contemporary to each other.

Timeline

B.C.

24,000   Potters of Dolni Vestonice (now in the Czech Republic) made small ceramic figurines, thought to have been used in rituals

10,500   Japanese invent pottery

9000–2500   Pottery is made in Africa, Europe, and Asia

8000   People in the Near East begin making sun-dried mud bricks to construct houses

6000   Pottery develops in the Near East

3500   Near Eastern potters begin to use turntables

3500–3250   Potter's wheel spreads to India, China, Japan, and Europe

2500–1000   Glazes are invented

600   In ancient Greece, ceramics becomes both an art and a profession

A.D.

700 Chinese invent porcelain and keep technique a secret for one thousand years

750 Islamic potters begin to develop unique styles

800s Luster glaze is invented by Islamic potters

1500s Europeans bring the potter's wheel to America

1708 Johann Friedrich Böttger creates porcelain

1800s Production of ceramics becomes industrialized; scientists discover that precious rubies are made of alumina, a chief ingredient in clay

1900s The Arts and Crafts Movement, born in England, spreads to the United States

1902 A. V. L. Verneuil creates synthetic gemstones

1930s Engineers learn to make microphones with piezo-electric ceramics

1941 R. B. Gray invents an advanced ceramic polycrystalline

1950s Silicon chips are invented

1960s Engineers begin to develop silicon nitride

1967 Bioceramics are invented

1974 Chinese peasants discover Emperor Qin's ceramic army

Glossary

advanced ceramics: materials that are not metals or plastics, and are not made of organic substances

bioceramics: ceramics that are compatible with the human body and are used in repairing or replacing body parts

Bioglass: a bioceramic made of glass, calcium, and phosphorus; used to make artificial bones for the ear

ceramics: (1) materials made of clay that has been mixed with water and then fired (heated to a high temperature) to make them permanently hard; (2) materials that are composed in large part of inorganic, nonmetallic materials (not metals or plastics, and are not made of organic substances); also known as *advanced ceramics*

ceramists: people who make ceramic articles

clay: a soft, malleable material that is rich in alumina silicates

coil construction: a method of making pottery in which the potter forms a flat piece of clay for the base of the pot, then rolls long, thin snakes of clay, forms them into circles, and places them one on top of another on the base

cubic zirconia: artificial gemstone made from molten zirconium oxide

delft: the Dutch and English name for tin-glazed pottery with a smooth white surface

earthenware: a reddish clay that hardens at relatively low kiln temperatures, is somewhat porous, and is often used for plates and bowls

faience: the French name for tin-glazed pottery with a smooth white surface

fireclays: clays with a high proportion of iron oxides used to make bricks

fired: heated to a high temperature

foot-wheel: a potter's wheel that is turned by kicking rather than with the hand

glazes: finely ground minerals suspended in a liquid that, when applied to the surface of ceramics and fired, give ceramics color and texture and seal their porous surfaces

Jomon pottery: the world's earliest pottery, made in Japan

kaolin: a white clay used to make porcelain

kilns: special ovens for firing pottery

luster: a glaze that incorporates metal and looks shiny or shimmery when fired

majolica: the Italian name for tin-glazed pottery with a smooth white surface

overglazes: glazes put on top of a primary glaze

piezoelectric ceramics: ceramics made of crystals that produce electricity when they are pressed

polycrystalline ceramic: an advanced ceramic made up of tiny crystals of barium, titanium, and oxygen or lead, zirconium, and oxygen; stronger than a piezoelectric ceramic

porcelain: a translucent, white ceramic that is made of kaolin and alabaster and is fired at high temperatures

Portland cement: a powder made from clay and limestone, which when mixed with water forms concrete

potsherds: broken pots

pottery: objects, such as pots and vases, that are made from ceramics

pyrometer: a kiln thermometer

pyrometric cones: conical triangular pieces of ceramic material that indicate by bending or melting that a certain temperature has been reached in a kiln

semiconductor: a ceramic material, used in the electronics industry, that allows some electricity to flow through it

silicon chip: also called *chip*; a piece of silicon that serves as the brains of computers, printers, and other electronic devices

silicon nitride: a ceramic material of silicon and nitrogen that is harder and lighter than steel

sintering: a process in which the molecules of silica and alumina in baking clay soften and collapse together to partially fill the spaces left by the water that has been driven off

slab construction: a method of making pottery in which a potter attaches flat pieces of clay to a base and to each other to form a clay object or container

slip: a soupy mixture of clay and water used to join pieces of clay together or smooth the surfaces of clay objects

studio potters: potters who make handcrafted pottery

terra-cotta: a reddish clay that hardens at relatively low kiln temperatures

transducer: a device that sends out sound waves via a piece of piezoelectric ceramic

turntable: a rotating circular platform on which a ceramic is placed to be shaped

vitrification: a process in which the molecules of silica in baking clay liquefy and form a noncrystalline, glassy substance that flows around the remaining alumina molecules

For Further Information

Camusso, Lorenzo, and Sandro Bortone, eds. *Ceramics of the World, From 4000 B.C. to the Present*. New York: Harry N. Abrams, Inc., 1991.

Gonen, Rivka. *Fired Up! Making Ceramics in Ancient Times*. Minneapolis: Runestone Press, 1993.

Richerson, David W. *The Magic of Ceramics*. Westerville, Ohio: The American Ceramic Society, 2000.

Index